TEXTILES

- a protection racket

This WORLD DEVELOPMENT MOVEMENT Report on Textiles focusses on the British Cotton and Allied Textile industry.

It calls for an end to the double-think of government , industrialists and trade unionists. Each pays lip service to its responsibilities to the poor countries[1] of the world. Yet each, in this case pursues policies which are inimicable to the interests of the mass of the people in those countries.

As the UK joins the enlarged European Economic Community the textile industry is clamouring for more protection against imports from poor countries.
Are its claims justified?
That depends how you look at them.
Take a glance and you see the hardy and long-suffering working men and women of Lancashire thrown out of work by the thousands as the British market is flooded with cheap textiles churned out in the sweat-shops of India, Pakistan and Hong Kong.

Look a little closer and you see an unresolved conflict between jobs for people in Britain and people in the poor countries.

Look closer still and you see a sordid succession of bluff, hypocrisy and double-think out of which neither successive British governments, nor the textile industry, nor some of the developing countries emerge with credit.

Trade restrictions

Producers of cotton textiles in the poor countries exporting to Britain have to overcome two forms of trade barrier:
● quotas or limits to the quantity of their goods they can sell in Britain. This means

TABLE 1
UK DOMESTIC CONSUMPTION (BY VOLUME) OF COTTON
AND ALLIED TEXTILE — BY SUPPLIER — including made-ups of cotton for 1955-60 India, Hong Kong Pakistan for 1969-71 split 2:1 for poor and rich countries

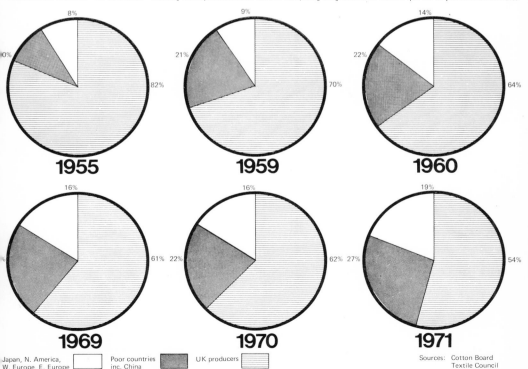

Japan, N. America, W. Europe, E. Europe | Poor countries inc. China | UK producers

Sources: Cotton Board Textile Council

that they are not allowed to sell as the consumer is willing to buy.

● tariffs or customs duty charged on their exports on entry into Britain. This means that the consumer has to pay more than the price the producer would be willing to sell at if the goods were not charged duty. (Cotton goods from Commonwealth countries such as India, Pakistan are charged duty at a slightly lower rate than those from non-Commonwealth countries, such as Taiwan, Brazil).

Producers of man-made textiles and textile mixtures such as polyester/cotton in poor countries exporting to Britain only face tariffs. They are, as yet, allowed to sell as much as they can after paying duty. But only a very small part of Britain's imports of these textiles come from developing countries.

The UK only imported about 27 per cent (by volume) of its total consumption of cotton and allied textiles[2] from poor countries in 1971[3].

Unlike the poor nations, the rich exporters of cotton textiles of Western Europe and North America only have one barrier to surmount. They only pay tariffs. They are allowed to sell as many cotton and allied textiles in Britain as they can, after paying customs duty.

Member countries of EFTA — the [4]European Free Trade Association — do still better. They are allowed to sell their textiles without even having to pay custom duty. Members of countries of the enlarged EEC —

European Economic Community — will be in the same happy position, facing neither quotas nor tariffs, from 1977.

These developed producers, plus other industrialized countries (Eastern bloc and Japan) supplied about 19 per cent of UK domestic consumption in 1971.

In short, cotton textiles produced in the poor countries are now discriminated against in two ways in Britain:

● They are charged customs duty — while textiles produced in the wealthier EFTA countries are not

● their sales are limited by quota — while textiles produced in Western Europe and North America are not.

There is in Britain today a vocal protectionist lobby, pioneered by the Textile Industry Support Campaign (TISC) now in league with the British Textile Employers' Association (BTEA) [5](a member of the British Textile Confederation (BTC).

It is pressing the UK government to extend this double discrimination immediately to man-made fibre goods. It is not alone. Through the activities of the European Affairs Committee of IFCATI — the International Federation of Cotton and Allied Textile Industries-trade associations in 13 other countries (including all the other members of the future European Community of Ten) are pressing their governments to impose both tariffs and quotas on cotton and allied textiles from poor countries.

The cotton industry's difficulties

Just after the Second World War the core of the cotton textile industry was made up of a large number of firms, many family owned, heavily concentrated in Lancashire.

Cotton textiles were an important component of Britain's industrial supremacy in the nineteenth and early twentieth centuries — a position bought, ironically, at the cost of the old Indian textile industry. [6] But by the early 1950's the cotton industry had lost many of its former export markets, including the newly independent countries of India and Pakistan which were expanding their own textile industries and competing with their old suppliers by exporting to the British market where they were able to sell cotton textile goods without paying duty under the arrangements known as Imperial

Preference. Table 1 shows how poor countries mainly India, Hong Kong and Pakistan doubled their share of the UK market in four years from 1955 to 1959.

Faced with contracting markets for their products both at home and abroad there were three alternatives facing Lancashire millowners; they could either

● reorganize the industry to compete effectively with the new textile producers

● demand protection and hang on

● give up and go out of business

The millowners claimed that in order to reorganize they needed some breathing space. To provide this, they demanded protection against rising imports from poor countries of

the Commonwealth.

This posed a problem for the government. It was unwilling to protect the sectional interests of the millowners, as there was a much greater consideration involved — Commonwealth trade. In any case the problems of the Lancashire cotton industry were not new. In 1946 a Board of Trade (BOT) working party had warned:

"The one thing that must be avoided is the enjoyment of this period (the anticipated post-war boom) as a fool's paradise of easy profits at the end of which the industry, and all those who rely on it for employment, may find themselves in worse difficulties than those of the inter-war years".[7]

It was like telling a child with a toffee not to suck it, in case it got tooth-ache.

In the three years 1949—51 the trading profits of publicly quoted cotton companies, averaged a third of their net assets. In 1951 profits were a staggering 39 per cent of net assets nearly twice the average of all quoted companies.

What did the cotton producers do with the money? Although they retained a greater proportion of their profits than the average company, they did not plough it back into buildings or machinery. [8] The BOT warning went unheeded. The working party had pointed to the need for new equipment, more modern production techniques, better marketing and wage negotiating machinery and radical changes in the industry's structure. But the millowners were too busy making money while they could, to care about securing employment for their workforce. In 1952 the bubble burst.[9]

The industry had sacrificed longer term stability for short-term gain. It is not therefore surprising that the government was sceptical about the industry's intentions, and evaded its demands for protection by urging the cotton companies to work out their own arrangements with textile producers in India, Pakistan and Hong Kong.

Keeping the poor out: voluntary quotas

The first attempt by the British industry to reach an understanding with Hong Kong producers failed in 1957. The British firms demanded a ceiling on the level of shipments for 3 years. The Hong Kong producers refused, pointing to their limited home market and their dependence on international trade. With the breakdown of talks with Hong Kong, a provisional agreement with India to exercise voluntary restraint, reached earlier in the year, also collapsed.

A second mission to Hong Kong in 1958 was more successful. After protracted discussions Hong Kong gave a voluntary undertaking to limit shipments to Britain from 1st February, 1959. This was followed by similar agreements with India and Pakistan. Having obtained 'voluntary' undertakings from the major suppliers of imported textiles to limit their shipments, the British industry had, ostensibly obtained a degree of market stability. It was then obliged to go through the motions of restructuring.

At the time the arrangements were made two new factors had altered the government's attitude towards the industry:

● new interest in Europe

● an impending general election

On the eve of the 1959 General Election, the Conservative government, sensitive about marginal Lancashire constituencies,[10] passed the Cotton Industry Act.[11]

The Act embodied three principal schemes:

● scrapping of spare and idle capacity

● re-equipment

● compensation for redundant workers.

Grants were offered to firms scrapping spare and idle capacity. These were financed two-thirds by the government and one-third by a levy on firms remaining in the industry. Higher grants were offered to firms who would scrap their plant and machinery and leave the industry altogether. The government was also to pay 25 per cent of the cost of new machinery. It was hoped these financial incentives would entice the industry to adopt the recommendations made 13 years previously by the 1946 Working Party.

The other important feature of the Act was the provision for compensating workpeople who lost their jobs as a result of either of the other schemes. They were more fortunate than those who lost their jobs in the industry prior to the Act. Between 1951 and 1959 employment in the cotton industry had fallen from 333,000 to 230,000 — a loss of 12,900 jobs a year.

Impact

Re-organisation and re-equipment were intended to make the industry competitive in the markets of the world, wherever standards of living were high. This emphasised the potential for easy-care and fashionable textiles which it was thought could be readily exploited by the home industry.[12]

But the incentives to persuade the industry to reorganise were evidently inadequate. the Government had estimated that £80—95 million would have to be spent on reequipment. Yet only three-fifths of this was eventually spent.

Less than a quarter of the small firms decided to give up and go out of business.[13]

Most of the mill-owners were more eager to cut their losses and hang on under an umbrella of protection than change the structure of the industry and improve its efficiency.

Even at this stage the British cotton industry had no legitimate complaint against poor countries. It consistently claimed that its share of the domestic market was being invaded by rising imports, of cloth from developing producers. But as Table 2 shows, this claim is baseless. In 1959 poor countries supplied 28 per cent of UK domestic consumption of cotton textiles, while the rich countries (Western Europe and Japan) only supplied 8 per cent. Within one year the rich countries' share had leapt to 15 per cent, while the poor countries edged forward to 29 per cent.

TABLE 2
UK DOMESTIC CONSUMPTION (BY VOLUME) OF COTTON TEXTILES
— BY SUPPLIER

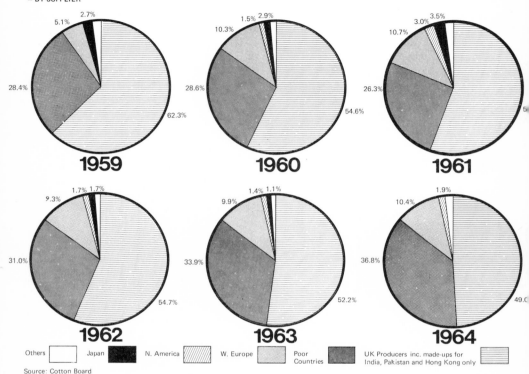

Source: Cotton Board

In the following year (1961) the rich countries' share grew even larger, to 17 per cent, while the poor countries' fell back to 27 per cent. It was not until 1962 that the poor countries regained part of the UK market from the rich, and 1963 that they made any substantial inroads at the expense of the UK producers.

Keeping the poor out: more voluntary quotas

By the early 1960's, the government had come round to the view that discriminatory controls would be needed on imports from India, Pakistan and Hong Kong, for the whole period of re-equipment and reorganization of the British industry, until 1964. So the 'voluntary' undertakings made by Hong Kong, India and Pakistan which expired, theoretically, in February 1962 and January 1963, were 'voluntarily' extended.

Letting the rich in
— European Free Trade Association
While the British textile industry had been prising 'voluntary' restrictions from India, Pakistan and Hong Kong, the UK government was negotiating the removal of barriers to trade between certain rich West European countries — the future members of the European Free Trade Association, which was formed in May, 1960. Customs duties on industrial products were to be progressively removed by the end of 1969. This timetable was eventually telescoped and duties were removed completely by 31st December, 1966. TABLE 3 shows the impact of that agreement on UK imports of cotton and allied textiles from EFTA countries.

One of the most striking features of the EFTA agreement was the inclusion of one-way preferences for Portugal. This country, in some respects an underdeveloped one, was permitted to retain its tariffs until 1972, while

Portuguese exports were granted free access to the markets of other EFTA members including Britain. Portugal subsequently became a significant supplier of cotton and other textiles to the British market.

It was a model of the sort of trade agreement between countries at different stages of economic development which has proved so difficult to achieve globally between rich and poor countries.

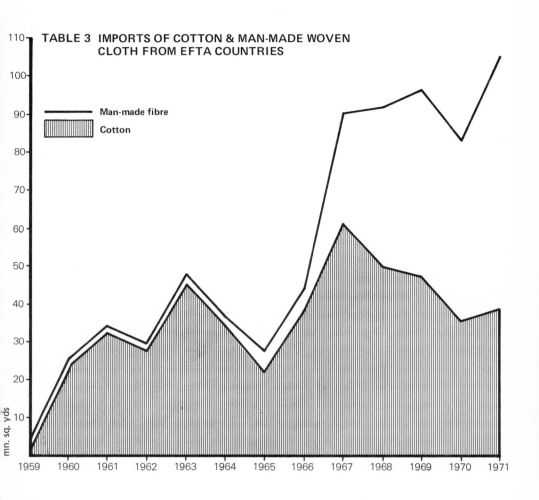

TABLE 3   IMPORTS OF COTTON & MAN-MADE WOVEN CLOTH FROM EFTA COUNTRIES

Man-made fibre

Cotton

mn. sq. yds

International discrimination

Meanwhile, developing producers of cotton textiles were beginning to be discriminated against in a new protectionist arrangement among the richer nations. In 1962, the wealthy members of the international trading club, the General Agreement on Tariffs and Trade (GATT) set up a Long Term Arrangement (LTA) under which they agreed to discriminate against textile imports from developing countries. This is still in force today: it comes up for renegotiation in 1973.

The LTA was ostensibly designed to increase the export earnings of poor countries enjoying a "natural" advantage in the production of cotton textiles by ensuring,

through quotas, a process of orderly marketing. Rich countries, who had been restricting imports from poor countries to low levels when the arrangement was drawn up, agreed to expand their quotas rapidly. Thus the Common Market countries agreed to increase quotas by 88 per cent per annum. Although this looks liberal, their imports from poor countries were too small for large percentage increases to make a great deal of difference unless continued for a long time.

The poor countries were hardly enthusiastic about the LTA:

India — 'the formula is the most widely

acceptable arrangement to help underdeveloped countries'.

Hong Kong — 'the outcome is not unsatisfactory as far as Hong Kong is concerned.'[14]

Furthermore even if a rich country thought its market would be disrupted it could unilaterally impose quotas against poor countries without let or hindrance.[15] They had set themselves up as judge, jury and executioner. For the poor countries there was no court of appeal.

Excuses

The rich countries claim the LTA is justified. They argue:

● that poor countries enjoy a **natural advantage** in the production of cotton textiles, either because they produce raw cotton, or have abundant supplies of cheap labour. In order to allow poor countries to exploit their 'natural' advantage a system of quotas was established to ensure ' orderly-marketing'; which means, in effect, to prevent disruption of the cotton textile industries established in the rich countries.

● that **disruption** was the inevitable consequence of the price advantage which their 'natural' advantage gave poor countries. Consider the situation from the point of view of a cotton textile manufacturer in a rich country. Low wages may reflect the lack of employment opportunities in poor countries. But as far as he is concerned low wages give them an 'unfair' advantage over him in pricing their goods. If they are allowed access to his home market they will simply take a larger and larger share. For him this means smaller and smaller production runs, dwindling profits and contracting employment. This trade with poor countries does not offer him reciprocal export opportunities in their markets compensating him for his losses at home. Therefore, unrestricted trade with poor countries is disruptive.
These views may be understandable from manufacturers and trade unionists. But they are also typical of governments in the rich countries.

● that the Government has to foot the bill for compensation paid to temporarily unemployed workers but it has to do this whatever the reason for their redundancy. But for consumers there are nothing but benefits to be had from being able to buy the cheapest goods available. There are also benefits for manufacturers and workpeople in other industries which stand to gain markets in poor countries for goods paid for with the proceeds of greater imports of textiles from those countries.

This more complex equation, which should justify a liberal attitude towards textiles imports from poor countries, was ignored in drawing up LTA. Instead, the Government of the rich countries bought the line the cotton textile manufacturers sold them.

One of the features of the LTA was provision for Austria, Denmark, Norway and Sweden and the Common Market countries to share out the burden of importing textiles by increasing the size of their quotas each year. Britain and Canada did not participate, although Britain did in fact agree to increase its quotas by 1 per cent each year, which because of the high level of imports meant, in absolute terms, greater access than that created by the larger percentage increases of the other countries. The object of burden-sharing was to make sure that at some point in the future each country would import a similar proportion of its cotton textiles consumption from poor countries. What was to happen then was never spelt out. There were two clear options. Either quotas could grow until poor countries supplied all cotton textiles; or quotas could be stabilized, each rich country taking a given proportion of cotton textiles from poor countries at some point in the future.

In fact the rich secretly thought that neither of these options would have to be taken. Technological breakthroughs were being made in the rich countries which would undermine the natural advantage of the poor

Rich pull barriers against poor — down UNCTAD

No sooner had the rich countries arranged international trade in cotton textiles to their own advantage than a major international initiative was launched to improve the trading prospects of poor countries. United Nations Conference on Trade and Development UNCTAD was born out of the deteriorating trade prospects of the poor world.[16] Its aim was to give preferential access for poor countries to the markets of the rich countries to persuade the rich countries unilaterally to open their markets to imports from underdeveloped countries, and to find ways of promoting them!

The most important outcome of the first UNCTAD in 1964 was a general resolution accepting in principle the need for poor countries to be given trade preferences.[17] The present British Prime Minister, Edward Heath — then President of the Board of Trade was partly responsible for endorsement of this resolution by the rich countries.

UK makes barriers against poor – Offical

Within a year of the UNCTAD conference the 'voluntarily' extended 'voluntary' quotas arrangements with India, Pakistan, Hong Kong and 32 other countries supplying relatively small quantities of cotton textiles to Britain were being systematically absorbed into an officially administered import quota scheme.

As far as the UK cotton industry had been concerned, the voluntary scheme had been a dismal failure. Quotas said the industry, had been set too high. However, it had been the industry itself which had reached the original agreement with the major suppliers; and from their introduction quotas were only filled half the time[18]

By 1965 imports of cotton cloth from Western Europe and North America were 26 per cent of all imports of cotton cloth compared with 15 per cent in 1959. Domestic producers were doing well; that year, they supplied 57 per cent of the domestic market, the largest share they had had since 1959.

Yet the industry intensified its efforts against imports from poor countries. It called for a higher tariff plus restriction on the volume and types of imports from all "low-cost" sources for a trial period of five to ten years.[19]

If the industry itself still not recognized its weaknesses there were others who did; the National Economic Development Council warned "some parts of the sector (cotton and allied textiles) are failing to compete effectively even with industries in other industrialized countries."[20]

In 1966, the year the quotas became official, 24 per cent of cotton cloth imported into UK was from Western Europe and North America. UK producers' share of the home market slipped back to 55 per cent. The fiction of the voluntary arrangements, originally agreed for three years for the industry to put itself in order, was over. **In 1966 the government, by then Labour controlled, gave in to pressure from the industry and took over complete adminis-tration of import quotas. Cotton textiles from poor countries were officially and openly discriminated against by the UK government.**

Changing cotton Industry

Meanwhile, the textile industry was changing. Developments such as new man-made fibres — synthetics (eg. polyesters) and different processing techniques (eg. knitting and non-woven fabrics.) Retailing innovations, the growth of mail order houses and multiple stores were intensifying demand for quality, competitively priced products.

In manufacturing a new group of giant firms emerged. Their rapid growth, during the 1960's, forced some of the structural change, which had been urged throughout the post-war period. Their strategy, of controlling production from fibre processing to marketing, offset the "natural" advantage of the poor countries.

The barriers reappraised

The 1969 report

Having agreed to administer quota protection the Government felt obliged to have another look at the British textile industry. In 1966 the Permanent Secretary to the Board of Trade, suggested to the Cotton Board that it undertake a major study to look into ways in which productivity and efficiency in the industry could be improved.

By the time the Report (Cotton and Allied Textiles: a report on present performance and future prospects) was published in 1969 the Cotton Board had become the Textile Council. The Report stated:

'It is evident that the fundamental cause of the industry's difficulties, and the reason why they have persisted so long, has been its failure to adjust to changing circumstances' (para. 561)

It went on:

'At present the UK industry is running to stay in the same place, and barely succeeding, if it is to catch up with its competitors it will have to run much faster'.

A shift in the industry's foreign trade performance will only come about, in fact, if major advances in productivity and efficiency can be achieved during the next few years'. (para 588)

In these respects it was echoing Caroline Miles, Lancashire Textiles, 1968, who stated:

"The view that imports have been and still are the sole cause of the industry's difficulties...... is a gross oversimplification."

The Report proposed the dismantling of quota restrictions and the introduction of a tariff on Commonwealth cotton textiles. It also forecast a drastic reduction in the number of (mills and weaving sheds) and separate firms. Employment in the industry was expected to contract by nearly half from 1968 to 75,000 in 1975.

Table 4 Cotton and allied textiles — proposed structure

	1961 After Act No. of Firms	1968 No of Firms	1975 No of Firms
Spinning		63	25-30
Weaving		279	100
Finishing		102	30
Total	**783**	**444**	**155-160**

Source: Textile Council

Restructuring was to be process of merger, bankrupcy or voluntary liquidation, as the creation of new groups from existing small and medium sized firms being left to private initiative'. The Report specifically rejected a 1959 type scheme financed part by the industry and part by government on the grounds that it would be a waste of public money. But it suggested special allowances similar to those available in Development Areas for investment in new buildings and machinery, and new depreciation allowances for multi-shift operated plants.

The Report's recommendations on trade policy meant both a further shift in Britain's attitude towards the Commonwealth, and a major change of opinion within the industry about the need for quotas to control textile imports from poor countries in the British market.

The Board of Trade had been associated with the Report from its inception. Not surprisingly, the Government announced, soon after it was published, that it accepted the gist of its findings. From the beginning of 1972, customs duties would be imposed on cotton textiles from Commonwealth countries and quotas would go. Imports of cotton and allied textiles from EFTA countries would continue to enter the British market free of duty.

Although the quotas on imports of textile goods from poor countries were to be removed, tariffs on them were to be consolidated by the proposed tariff on Commonwealth suppliers.

In his statement to the House of Commons, announcing the new measures on 22nd July,

1969 the President of the Board of Trade, Mr. Anthony Crosland, at last recognized that if anyone had benefitted from discriminatory quotas it had been other rich countries.

"The effect of the new arrangement should be to reduce imports from developed (rich) countries, which have benefitted markedly from the existence of quota restrictions on imports from developing (poor) countries."

He went on;

"There is no reason to think that with the possible exception of India, the developing countries of the Commonwealth generally will be able to export less to Britain over a tariff of this amount than they would be under a continuation of the quota system."[21]

The developing countries were less sanguine. Reaction in India was particularly hostile. There was a call for retaliatory measures: nationalisation of British interests, and a 15 per cent tariff on British exports to India.[22] In a booklet published later in 1969 cotton interests in India claimed a drastic drop would occur in India's foreign exchange from cotton textile exports to Britain of £16½m.[23] It was reported that Hong Kong was angered by the failure of the British negotiate before announcing the tariff and it predicted that the Commonwealth share of the British market would be taken over by Britain's EFTA partners.[24]

Meanwhile, opinion in the textile industry was divided on the new proposals. Asked how the decision would be received in Lancashire Antony Crosland had said "it will be welcomed by all the most progressive elements on both sides of industry."

An editorial in the Times Business News next day commented, "The imposition of a tariff will be welcomed in Lancashire, but it will only serve its purpose if Lancashire regards it less as protection than as a challenge."[25] Two days after the proposals were announced, the British Textiles Employers Association BTEA, commented that there should be a limited transitional period of double protection (against poor countries) of quotas and tariffs.

Attached to the Textile Report itself was a Note of Dissent by Mr. Edmund Gartside, a Lancashire mill-owner. He stated bluntly:

"I believe the fundamental cause of the industry's problems is imports.....unless more positive action is taken than is recommended in the Report, the remainder of the Report becomes almost irrelevant"[26]

This minority view was diametrically opposed to the mainstream of thinking in the Report. This was that quotas tend to inhibit the process of restructuring, and the achievement of international competitiveness, as they guarantee bits of the market for UK producers, however high their costs compared with other overseas producers.

Whereas tariff protection weeds out very high cost producers and acts as an incentive for progressive firms to undertake the regrouping and restructuring necessary to make the industry competitive against allcomers.

That Mr. Gartside's view might have supporters in Lancashire should have been clear from a paragraph in the main Report which warned:

'Unless a sufficient number of units (factories) and firms go out of business, the movement towards higher investment

and increased shift working will be hindered and progress towards the goal of a compact and viable industry effectively retarded'.[27]

Already, the mill-owners were suffering from a credit squeeze and a shortage of capital for new investment.[28] They took little advantage of offers of assistance from the IRC, which had made £10 million available in loans for construction and equipment for either new factories or complete modernization, and was anxious to promote mergers between small and medium-sized firms. Nearly a year after the proposals were announced, the Textile Council urging more mergers, warned,

"some companies, at present, hanging on in the Micawber like hope of something turning up, will not be able to survive the harsh realities of the post-1972 situation."

With just over one year to go to the changeover from quotas to tariff the industry was faced with another problem — inflation began to drive up costs.[29]

In its final lament, the Textile Council remarked, sadly,

"the clear implication is that re-equipment and modernization have proceeded less rapidly than was hoped by the authors of the Report (1969). To the extent that this is true the industry is less well placed to meet the challenge posed by the abolition of quotas on 1st January, 1972, not to mention the subsequent progressive reduction of tariffs in the likely event of this country's entry into the Common Market (EEC)".[30]

One thing is clear. It was not imports from poor countries which were to blame for the industry's continuing difficulties. For during 1969 and 1970 domestic producers gained a larger share of the market for cotton and allied textiles.

The government's volte-face

It was only time before the industry succeeded in forcing the government to change its mind about switching tariffs for quotas.

In the Autumn of 1971 a group of local-based employers' associations and the trade unions joined forces and launched the Textile Industry Support Campaign — (TISC) under the chairmanship of Mr. Edmund Gartside. With a substantial budget of £30,000 TISC employed the services of a public relations firm and saturated the media with dire warnings of rising unemployment in the textile areas, an increasing number of mill closures and the impending collapse of the cotton and allied textile industry, unless the

government took positive action to control—imports.

The government held fast. In the House of Commons Mr. Anthony Grant, Under-Secretary of State for Trade and Industry, said,

"Those who predict disaster for Lancashire should keep things in perspective.... Any increase in unemployment is a matter of concern, but even in the textile belt of Lancashire unemployment is not primarily a textile problem.... There is also evidence that overseas suppliers have held their prices steadier than UK producers, whose prices rose by about 20 per cent between

1968 and 1970.... Four-fifths of the increase in imports of woven fabrics of man-made fibres come from European and North American sources, not from low-cost suppliers."[31]

Within ten days the government did what any other group of hard-headed, short-sighted politicians would do. It capitulated.

On 8th December, 1971 the Secretary of State for Trade and Industry, Mr. John Davies announced that quotas on imports of cotton textiles from poor countries would be retained for another year.[32] With the proposed tariff on Commonwealth suppliers being imposed from 1 January 1972, double protection against cotton textile imports from poor countries was on.

Whilst TISC made a great deal of noise, it is doubtful whether it was instrumental in the government's change of policy. The powerful voices in the industry are the large firms, Courtaulds, Carrington Viyella, English Calico. Behind the scenes, they must have lobbied for a change in government policy. For them the key consideration was the enlarged EEC. Free trade in textile goods in the Common Market exists in theory, but not in practice. Determined customs officials are more effective than any tariff or quota in keeping textiles out of their countries. The large companies feared that in discriminating, customs officials would keep them out of EEC markets, because of Britain's position as a large importer "cheap"

textiles from poor countries. By retaining quotas the government did the window-dressing necessary to placate their fears.

The Government's decision to retain double protection was a bad decision. It was bad for three reasons.

● There is nothing in this change of policy to give fresh hope to the British operatives who either have lost or will lose their jobs in the cotton and allied textile industry. No policies to provide alternative job opportunities. No additional financial benefits to compensate them for the non-availability of work.

● It used poor countries as a scapegoat. UK producers lost part of their home market to both poor countries and rich countries in 1971. Although imports of cotton cloth and made-ups from poor countries di rise in 1971 from the low levels of 1970, these were permitted increases within quota limits. Imports from Western Europe and North America, not controlled by quotas rose by 15 per cent from 122.9m sq. yds. in 1970 to 141.0m sq. yds.

● It gave fuel to protectionist elements in the textile industry in the UK and Europe, as well as other industries, such as footwear, and gloves. No sooner had the government given in on cotton textiles than the TISC started to demand double protection against man-made fibres from poor countries as well.

The unemployment myth

The Lancashire textile industry has not only had to endure the buffets of changing fashion and of world trade. It has been adversely affected by the development of man-made fibres and new processing techniques such as knitting and non-woven and bonded fabrics. It is a declining sector of the UK textile industry, providing one-tenth of the jobs in 1971 compared with one-sixth in 1963.

In the first quarter of 1972 it provided employment for 91,150 people. This represents a massive reduction of jobs compared with 1951 when the industry employed over 333,000 people. (See Table 5). Those people did not disappear. The one impressive thing about the run-down of the Lancashire industry is that unlike other areas at one time heavily dependent upon one particular industry for employment, eg. the Clyde and shipbuilding, it has never resulted in massive and intractable unemployment. Jobs have been lost at the rate of over

11,000 a year since 1951. Despite this the level of unemployment in the traditional textile areas has not until recently been out of step with the national average. Even now there is no direct correlation between the jobs lost in textiles and higher unemployment levels.

There is one reason: availability of alternative jobs. Determined efforts have been made in Lancashire to diversify employment. Those displaced from the textile industry have gone into other industries offering better pay and conditions. During the 1960's there were even reports of a labour shortage in the industry.[33]

By mid-1971, less than 4 per cent of jobs in the North-West employment region were in the textile industry. True, this low figure obscures concentrations in certain towns, for example, Nelson — 30 per cent, Oldham — 10 per cent.[34]

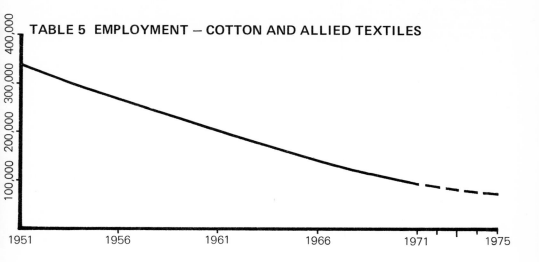

TABLE 5 EMPLOYMENT — COTTON AND ALLIED TEXTILES

In 1971 the labour force in textiles in Lancashire fell by about 11,500, but unemployment in the industry increased by only 2000. Most of those becoming redundant clearly either found new jobs or withdrew from the labour force.[35] The TISC claims further contraction in the industry will mean high unemployment in Lancashire. This would appear to be exaggerated.

Britain's policy towards textiles from poor Commonwealth countries has undoubably contributed to the decline in employment in the industry. But the weight of evidence is that the industry, that is the employers, have consistently failed over the past 25 years to come to terms with the prevailing market conditions. It is their failings which have put at risk the livelihoods of those workpeople who, throughout the post-war period, have depended on the cotton and allied textile industry for employment.

It is evident that in 1971 the trade unions were faced with an acute dilemma. From a long term point of view they knew that employment in the industry had to contract. They had been involved in the Textile Council Report which forecast this. On the other hand they could not stand idly by faced with a government which had proved unable to create enough jobs for people whose redundancies were anticipated in a Report published over two years ago.

So they joined TISC, even though they recognised that what Lancashire really needed and still needs is more diversification, not the retention of textiles for textiles' sake.[36]

In any event protection for textiles will not provide secure employment. The stark logic of the Textile Council Report was that unless the massive restructuring it recommended

took place, the industry's ability to compete and provide employment even for an estimated workforce of 75,000 by 1975 would be jeopardized.

This was borne out by the activities of the major companies in the industry. In 1971, although they improved their profits all of them cut back their labour force in the cotton and allied sector.

In his annual report, 1971/72 Carrington Viyella's Chairman, Mr. Jan Lewando welcomed the government's decision to retain quotas with tariffs — a policy which he said had regard for the employment situation. His company made 2000 people in the cotton and allied sector redundant in 1971.[37]

English Calico's Chairman, Mr. Neville Butterworth at a Press conference announcing his company's 1972 results was more two faced. It would be a tragedy if the British Textile Industry were dismantled further, he said adding, "The great blessing in our industry is its workforce. They are absolutely splendid."[38] His company reduced its labour force by one fifth in 1971 — over 4000 jobs lost.

Courtauld's chairman, Lord Kearton made no publicly recorded reference to the change of policy. Though according to a shareholder at the Annual General Meeting, 1972 some of the TISC arguments were expressed. Courtaulds reduced their labour force in the cotton and allied sector by about 2000 in 1971. The other major company with interests in the sector Coats Paton also reduced its labour force.

So the loss of employment due to the activities of these four companies alone accounts for over 70 per cent of the jobs lost in the industry in 1971.

11

British consumers ignored

In the whole affair consumer interests have been ignored for considerations of employment and domestic producers' markets. Should consumers have to pay for expensively produced British cotton textiles when cheaper goods of comparable quality are available from producers in poor countries? Retail chains and mail order firms, such as British Home Stores and Littlewoods think not; and it is not that they are being charitable to poor countries, if the right goods were available at the right price and quality they would buy British.

For many types of textiles, worsteds, knitwear jersey fabrics and warp knits, British producers excel in quality and price. They are not so good at making other textile products — shirting, corduroy and towellings, for example. In some instances the manufacturing capacity simply does not exist in Britain. **At the time when the rising cost of living is posing considerable difficulties for lower paid workpeople it is monstrous to protect high-cost textile manufacturers, improving their profitability with marginal, if any, gains in employment.**[39]

Common Market barriers

With Britain's entry into the EEC tariffs on textile trade in the enlarged Community will be removed by 1st July, 1977. At present 5 per cent of Britain's consumption of cotton and allied textiles is supplied by the Community of Six despite the tariffs 17.5 per cent on cotton fabrics. The Textile Council has already questioned the ability of the British industry to compete in the enlarged community.

Even before the new members of the enlarged EEC have formally joined the Community, agreement has been reached between the enlarged Community and the remaining members of EFTA on the creation of a Western European Free Trade Area, which includes every country except Spain.

This will mean free trade in textiles. between each of the member countries. About 12 per cent of UK domestic consumption of cotton and allied is imported from those countries.

Textile producers are pressing for quota restrictions to be extended to cover man-made fibres as well as cotton textiles and knitted as well as woven fabrics. British producers are pressing for a fairer distribution of imports from poor countries among all the members of the enlarged Community. It is a ploy which may be self-defeating. Taking all textile fabrics and clothing imports together, by value, West Germany imports more from poor countries than Britain both absolutely and per capita (see Table 6)

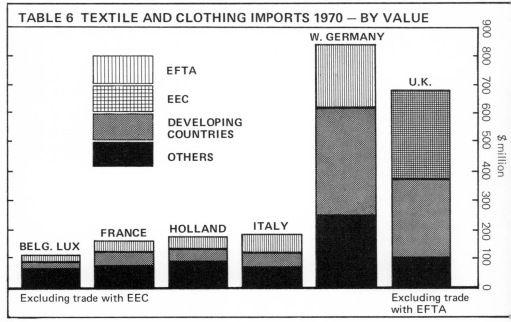

TABLE 6 TEXTILE AND CLOTHING IMPORTS 1970 — BY VALUE

All the member states of the Community of Six have different import quotas for cotton textiles. The Six have also included cotton textiles within their General Preference Scheme, unlike the UK. Their preferences, in the form of limited duty-free quota within the import quotas, are extended to eight developing countries: India, Pakistan, South Korea, Taiwan, Mexico, Brazil, United Arab Republic and Jamaica. The concession is geared to the level of imports from those countries into each member of the Community in 1968.

The Commission would like to liberalise this scheme, gradually abandoning import quotas for tariff preferences over the next five years. Large scale contraction in employment is occurring in the whole textile industry in the EEC, as it is in Britain. It has been estimated that 30,000 to 40,000 workpeople are leaving the industry here every year. The Commission recommends that the European Social Fund should be used to retrain these workpeople.[40]

It is highly doubtful whether these proposals will find a champion on the Council of Ministers. The refreshing thing about them is that they do not endorse the view held in most official quarters that textile imports from poor countries have a more than proportionally disruptive effect on established textile industries in the rich countries. The Commission accepts that the Community has an obligation to import manufactured goods from poor countries. They realize the key to fulfilling this obligation is designing the right domestic policies. But the Commission is not subject to the same political pressure as the national governments.

A recent policy paper issued by the WDM on Textile Trade policy in the enlarged EEC asked the British government to press for the same access for textiles from poor countries as the members of the enlarged

community will grant the remaining members of EFTA. This meant free access for poor countries from 1st July, 1977.

The government replied that whilst in principle free access was a desirable objective, the timing was out of the question. Furthermore it insisted that imports from poor countries have a more than proportionally disruptive effect on British Industry. They discounted WDM's view that improvements in productivity and the development of new fibres and processing techniques have had a much greater disruptive impact on employment in cotton and allied textiles, than imports from poor countries. [41] This must be regarded as an indication that Britain will in fact follow other rich countries in not only renegotiating the GATT Long Term Arrangement for cotton but for man-made fibre textiles as well.

Pressure is being imposed on Western European governments by man-made fibre interests for an extension of quotas. The United States has already obtained 'voluntary' quota arrangements on man-made textiles from Far-East Asian producers. Discriminatory protection against cotton and allied textiles throughout the 1970's seems inevitable.

Yet when Britain's overall trading position in all textile and clothing is considered. In 1971 there was a favourable balance of £52m. (see Table 7).

Admittedly there was an unfavourable balance with poor countries, but so there was with the Common Market. Both were more than compensated for by sale in other markets.

On the other side of the coin Britain had a favourable balance of trade in machinery and transportation equipment with poor countries of over £1,000 million in 1971! It might have been more if we had bought a few more textiles!

Table 7 UK Trade in Textiles and clothing — by value 1971

TC	EEC		EFTA		Poor countries (excluding China)		Total £000's	
	Imports	Exports	Imports	Exports	Imports	Exports	Imports	Exports
5 Textile Fabrics	84709	60348	85416	109232	73510	72540	324938	425825
4 Clothing	17374	21658	40921	44019	85108	15242	178200	129485
TOTALS	102083	82006	126337	153251	158618	87782	503138	555310
BALANCE	-20077		+26914		-70836		+52172	

Source: UK Overseas Trade Statistics

Why it all matters

If the poor countries are to have any hopes of obtaining export opportunities, not greater than, but the same as those the rich are creating for each other and a fair deal from GATT — the double dealing of the rich countries must end. Cotton and Allied Textiles is a test case for the countries of the rich world. About 80 per cent of the poor countries' foreign exchange earnings are from sales of commodities: industrial raw materials and foodstuffs. These have less growth potential than sales of manufactures. The return on processing both in terms of employment and foreign exchange earnings is very much greater.

What was the price you paid for the last cotton shirt or blouse you bought? Compare it with the value of the raw cotton which was processed to make up your shirt or blouse; that was worth about 7½ pence. A few poor countries have established some industries which are competitive with industries in the rich countries. From the point of view of the future of poor countries it is as important — perhaps more important — that those industries are encouraged to grow, than that their markets for sugar and coffee, for which there is limited growth, are expanded.

Cotton and allied textiles is the one major industry in which some poor countries have achieved international competitiveness.

And the rich have deprived them of access to their fastest growing markets. They intend to continue doing so.

The UK government, despite the charges that have been levelled against it, can and must take the opportunity of discussions in the enlarged EEC to end this protection racket against poor countries.

Quotas are superfluous for the companies which have effectively restructured themselve and for workpeople who need jobs.

Tariffs mean the customer has to pay more than he need do. It should be possible to obtain trade union support. Multinational corporations, are not involved in the product ion of textiles in poor countries, as they are in the case of electronics for example. The job opportunities which will be created in poor countries through trade, will eventually push up the low wages currently paid in those countries.

These reflect the lack of employment opportunities rather than exploitation of cheap labour where trade union rights are suppressed, as they are for example in Portugal. This initiative must also be followe by each of the member governments of the enlarged Common Market. Then the textile producers in poor countries could enjoy trading opportunities in the Common Marke equal to those enjoyed by every Western European country (except Spain). It is not a matter of granting preferential treatment.

What must be done

The WDM therefore calls for:
(1)   the members of the enlarged EEC to expand their individual import quotas until they become redundant by 1st July, 1977.

(2)   the UK to abandon her quota scheme from 1st January, 1973.

(3)   the expansion of the EEC Generalized Preference Scheme of tariff-quotas and their geographical coverage until they extend duty-free access to all the present beneficiaries of the UK General Preference Scheme.

(4)   the reduction of UK tariffs against all

beneficiaries of its General Preference Schem

If any member government fails to compensate adequately workpeople made redundant, or to stimulate and provide adequate jobs in areas where structural unemployment might become a problem through the impact of this trade liberalisatio It should be obliged to suffer the political consequences, and not be allowed to use developing countries as scapegoats for its inadequate domestic policies. **These measure would only make a small contribution to the development efforts of the Third World but it would be a move in the right direction.**

Footnotes

The expression — 'poor countries' is used to emphasize that although they may be developing, those countries are still poor relative to ours, so are the mass of their people. They are taken as all those countries included in Schedule 1, Part 1 of the Import Duties (Developing Countries) Order, 1971 i.e. (beneficiaries of the UK General Preference Scheme) plus the People's Republic of China.

Cotton is no longer considered in isolation from its man-made fibre substitutes which are spun and woven like cotton, sometimes in mixtures hence cotton and allied textiles

The major suppliers are India, Pakistan and Hong Kong.

Sweden, Norway, Denmark, Switzerland, Austria, Portugal, Finland and Iceland.

TISC Newsletter, July 1972.

Peter Donaldson, Worlds Apart, BBC, London 1971, pp 27-28.

Board of Trade Working Party Report: HMSO, London 1946, p. 194.

Caroline Miles, Lancashire Textiles. CUP, 1968, p 29. During this period there was a shortage of machinery in Britain, 90 per cent of production was being exported, with Government encouragement, to assist the balance of payments.

Labour was even imported during this boom-period to man spare capacity. Despite good relations between employers and trade unions the employers' failure to heed the BOT working party recommendations jeopardized future employment in the industry.

The Times, 25th September 1959.

Board of Trade, Reorganization of the Cotton Industry, Cmmd 744 (1959)

C. Miles, op. cit p.48.

C. Miles op. cit p. 56.

Far Eastern Economic Review 1st March, 1962.

GATT, Basic Instruments and Selected Documents, 11th Supplement, 1962.

16 Peter Adamson, UNCTAD III — Make or break for Development, WDM, 1971.

17 Kam Hameed, Preferences — A Better Deal for the Poor World? WDM, 1972

18 C. Miles, op. cit., p.80

19 Cotton Board, The Case for a viable UK cotton industry, Manchester, 1964.

20 National Economic Development Council, Imported Manufactures — an inquiry into competitiveness, London, 1965.

21 Hansard 22nd July 1969, col 1507.

22 The Times, 29th July 1969.

23 India's Case — New Textile Policy of UK, Indian Cotton Mills' Federation, Bombay, 1969. p. 18.

24 The Times 23rd July, 1969.

25 The Times, 23rd July 1969.

26 Textile Council: Cotton and Allied Textiles, Manchester 1969. p. 131.

27 Textile Council, ibid, paragraph 537.

28 Times, 24th November, 1969.

29 The Times, 3rd November, 1970.

30 Textile Council, Review No. 38, July/ July 1971 p. 12.

31 Hansard, 29th November 1971, col. 215ff.

32 Hansard, 8th December, 1971, col. 1305.

33 Caroline Miles op. cit p. 84.

34 R. Naylor, Social Consequences of Textile Industry Contraction, TISC, 1972.

35 Hansard, 29th November, 1971, col 215ff.

36 Hansard 14th December, 1971, col. 405.

37 Daily Telegraph, 4th April, 1972.

38 Financial Times, 1st March, 1972.

39 Financial Times, 1st March, 1972.

40 European Community, October 1971.

41 See ILO Textile Committee Report, 1968.